HOW YOUth TRIUMPH IN SPORTS

TOOLS THAT CREATE A TRIUMPHANT LIFE

WORKBOOK

MICHELLE MORGAN

Copyright © 2021 Michelle Morgan

All rights reserved. No part of this publication may be reproduced, distributed, or transmitted in any form or by any means, including photocopying, recording, or other electronic or mechanical methods, without the prior written permission of the author, except in the case of brief quotations embodied in critical reviews and certain other noncommercial uses permitted by copyright law.

Books may be purchased for educational, business, or sales promotional use. For information please contact the author.

The author may be contacted at:
Website: www.VidaEsOro.org
Instagram, Twitter and Facebook: @VidaEsOro

ISBN-13 for this workbook: 978-0-9977978-4-8
ISBN for the book: 978-0-9977978-3-1

DEDICATION

This book is dedicated to all the young people who have a vision and a plan and to those who think they don't. You have the choice to create your life and your life is full of abundant possibilities and opportunities. At any moment you can decide to change the path you're on. Your mindset and your actions will create your destination.

If you're reading this, you have more light to be sharing and shining amongst others. You are worth more than you know!

Treasure Yourself & Shine

How YOUth Triumph in Sports: Tools That Create a Triumphant Life can easily be connected to the National Physical Education Standards.

*Standard 1: The physically literate individual demonstrates competency in a variety of motor skills and movement patterns.

Standard 2: The physically literate individual applies knowledge of concepts, principles, strategies and tactics related to movement and performance.

Standard 3: The physically literate individual demonstrates the knowledge and skills to achieve and maintain a health-enhancing level of physical activity and fitness.

Standard 4: The physically literate individual exhibits responsible personal and social behavior that respects self and others.

Standard 5: The physically literate individual recognizes the value of physical activity for health, enjoyment, challenge, self-expression and/or social interaction.

*Advanced Solutions International, Inc. (n.d.). National PE Standards. Retrieved from https://www.shapeamerica.org/standards/pe/

To find the Physical Education Standards for your state, you may access them on the following link: https://www.shapeamerica.org/advocacy/advocacyresources_state.aspx

TABLE OF CONTENTS

Preface 9

Introduction 11

Why Do You Play? 12

Goals 15

Focus Calendar 17

Education 22

Accountability 24

Being Coachable 30

Know Your Worth 33

Mental Toughness 35

Character Counts 40

Believe 46

PREFACE

What was your initial reaction when you saw the cover of the book? I want to let you know that this book is dedicated to you, literally, read the dedication page. This book is bigger than sports, the words that you read are all about you creating your life. The life you've envisioned with abundance, genuine love, genuine happiness, and fun. You can use the tools that are shared to you in this book to reach your full potential in life. You were born to be great, you were born with a gift to share with The Universe.

You may be thinking, "I don't know what my gift is," and that's okay. As you go through the book, listen to the words as you read them, connect and you may hear your gift speaking to you.

For those of you who don't play sports, where you may see the word basketball or another sport, insert what you love doing and/or love learning about, or what you're working towards earning. For example, you may insert cooking, artist, gardener, computers, student, scientist, engineer, teacher, business owner, and so on.

How YOUth Triumph in Sports is a book about the important traits I learned through sports and the value they can hold throughout the course of your life. Although, I am sharing what has supported me in triumphing in my life, it is ultimately up to you to put the action and effort into applying them into your life.

In anything you do, the choice is yours. The choices you make will determine the direction your journey will take.

POSITIVE CHARACTER TRAITS

Accountable	Adaptable	Adventurous	Alert	Ambitious	Appropriate
Assertive	Astute	Attentive	Authentic	Aware	Bravery
Calm	Candid	Capable	Certain	Charismatic	Clear
Collaborative	Committed	Communicator	Compassion	Comradeship	Connected
Conscious	Considerate	Consistent	Contributes	Cooperative	Courageous
Creative	Curious	Dedicated	Determined	Diplomatic	Directive
Disciplined	Dynamic	Easygoing	Effective	Efficient	Empathetic
Empowers	Energetic	Enthusiastic	Ethical	Excited	Expressive
Facilitates	Fairness	Faithful	Fearless	Flexible	Friendly
Generative	Generosity	Gratitude	Happy	Hard Working	Honest
Honorable	Humorous	Imaginative	Immaculate	Independent	Initiates
Innovative	Inquiring	Inquiring	Integrates	Integrity	Intelligent
Intentional	Interested	Intimate	Joyful	Knowledgeable	Leading
Listener	Lively	Logical	Loving	Loyal	Manages Time Well
Networker	Nurturing	Open-Minded	Optimism	Organized	Patient
Peaceful	Planner	Playful	Poised	Polite	Powerful
Practical	Presents Self Well	Proactive	Problem-Solver	Productive	Punctual
Reliable	Resourceful	Responsible	Self-confident	Self-generating	Self-reliant
Sense of Humor	Sensual	Serves Others	Sincere	Skillful	Spiritual
Spontaneous	Stable	Strong	Successful	Supportive	Tactful
Trusting	Trustworthy	Truthful	Versatile	Vibrant	Warm
Willing	Wise	Zealous			

INTRODUCTION

Who are you? This is a question you may have asked yourself before or maybe you haven't. There are days when you may be certain you know and feel confident about who you are and there may be days when you have doubted yourself or don't know. I have felt all of these emotions as well, so know you're not alone. Although, there have been days of uncertainty about myself, below is a tool that I use so that I always remember who I am.

On the spaces provided you're going to write your name and you're going to select three positive words that describe who you are. On the previous page there are examples of positive descriptive words that you may choose from or you're more than welcome to come up with your own. After each "I am", write in one of the words you have chosen.

MY NAME IS _____

I AM _____

I AM _____

I AM _____

This is your declaration of who you are. When times get a little tough or when you're feeling great, say this out loud or to yourself as a reminder that you're capable of achieving anything that you put your mind to. The only person who needs to validate what you're saying is YOU! As long as you believe it, then you will continue to exude it through your actions, words, and energy. You can change the words at any time or add some new ones.

Say this everyday and shine your light!

WHY DO YOU PLAY?

You must know your "Why" in everything you do regardless if it's in sports or in life. Your "Why" is the foundation to setting your goals in all that you do.

Exercise: Write down 1-3 goals that you have in any area of your life. After each goal write down why you want to achieve each goal. Sometimes we think the reason we want to achieve a goal is based off one particular "Why", but really it goes further than that. After you respond with your first "Why", ask "Why" a second time to that response and continue the pattern until you've gone at least 3 levels down. If you feel you can go further, then please do so.

Example:
Goal 1: I will earn a basketball scholarship.
Why? I love playing basketball and want to play in college and earn a free education.
Why? I have 5 sisters and I don't want my parents to have to worry about paying for me to go to college.
Why? I want my parents to save their money and use it towards other things since opportunities exist for me to obtain a free education.
Goal 2: Own my own business working with youth in sports.
Why? I've been in their shoes as a student-athlete and want to give back with the lessons I've learned.
Why? For me, giving back goes beyond sports. Life is happening outside of sports: in our homes, communities, work environments, etc. How we feel and react to situations can affect how we move forward towards our goals.
Why? I want to provide a safe space for young people to voice their feelings without judgement in order to grow and learn from the experiences they've had.

Goal 1:_____

Why?_____

_____

Why?_____

_____

Why?_____

_____

Goal 2:_____

Why?_____

_____

Why?_____

_____

Why?_____

_____

Goal 3:_____

Why?_____

_____

Why?_____

_____

Why?_____

_____

Circle of Support (C.O.S.)

These are the people who you speak openly and honestly to when you're feeling great or on days where you don't feel motivated. These are also the people who give you honest feedback, even if it's something that you don't want to hear, it may be what you need to hear at that time. Your Circle of Support are people who know what your "Why" is and have listened to the vision you want to create for your life. If you don't share the details with them, how are they going to know how to support you with guidance, resources, and/or words of encouragement.

Remember, to keep an open mind when feedback is given to you, we'll touch more on this in a later part of the book.

Name the people who are in your Circle of Support (C.O.S.)

1._____

2._____

3._____

4._____

5._____

Reach out to the people you listed and let them know they're in your Circle of Support. Tell them what your C.O.S. represents and share with them your vision for your life and possibly anything that's on your mind.

GOALS

At the beginning of the book, you wrote down goals you wanted to achieve along with your "Why." At this point we're going to create long and short-term goals that relate to the goals you stated earlier. Refer back to the chapter, "Why Do You Play?" and determine the time frame you're going to use. Remember, these are examples on how to set long and short-term goals, there is no right or wrong way to set them. Set your time frames and goals to best suit you for accomplishing them and you can always adjust them as needed.

Example:
Long-Term Goal: Earn a college basketball scholarship (Let's assume I'm a freshman in high school when I wrote this. This would be a 4-year goal when I graduate from high school).
Short-Term Goal: Here, I would break my goals into different segments: pre-season, regular season, playoffs, and the off-season. Below is an example of my short-term goals during the season.

On Mondays, Wednesdays, and Fridays I will commit to making 250 shots inside the 3-point line, making 250 shots from the 3-point line, and making 150 free throws. On Tuesdays and Thursdays, I will commit to working on my ball handling for an hour. Finally, on Saturdays and Sundays I will commit to making 500 jump shots inside the 3-point line and from the 3-point line, along with making 300 free throws. I will also improve on my ball handling skills for an hour. I will also stay committed to completing all assignments for school and study for quizzes and tests, as I will need to have good grades in order to continue playing on my current team as well as in college.

Below is an example of how to use the Focus Calendar when creating goals like the example above.

Long-Term Goal: Create and run my own business working with youth in sports.

Short-Term Goals:

Week 1: I will create my business name, mission statement, purchase a domain name, and create social media accounts.

Week 2: Network and connect with other business owners, ask questions, take notes, learn best practices and come up with a plan of action on how to move forward as a business owner in my field.

... FOCUS CALENDAR ...

Month: MAY

My Goal for this Month is: BEGIN TO BUILD MY OWN BUSINESS

This Week I Will Focus On...	MONDAY	TUESDAY	WEDNESDAY	THURSDAY	FRIDAY	SATURDAY	SUNDAY	Did I accomplish my tasks for this week? What did I learn this week and how can I improve?
CREATE: BIZ NAME, MISSION STATEMENT, SOCIAL MEDIA ACCOUNTS, PURCHASE DOMAIN NAME	CREATE BIZ NAME ①	PURCHASE DOMAIN NAME ②	CREATE MISSION STATEMENT ③	COMPLETE MISSION STATEMENT ④	CREATE SOCIAL MEDIA ACCOUNTS ⑤	COMPLETE ANY UNFINISHED TASKS ⑥	COMPLETE ANY UNFINISHED TASKS ⑦	I'M STILL WORKING ON MY MISSION STATEMENT; BE MORE ORGANIZED
NETWORK AND CONNECT WITH OTHER BUSINESS OWNERS	NETWORKING MIXER 5-7PM ⑧	MEET WITH JAY 12-1PM ⑨	CHAMBER OF COMMERCE MIXER 5:30-8PM ⑩	MEET WITH NOAH 8AM-8:45AM ⑪	MEET WITH EMMA 11:45AM-1PM ⑫	FOLLOW UP WITH PEOPLE I MET ⑬	⑭	EMMA HAD TO RESCHEDULE; NEED TO MAKE BUSINESS CARDS FOR NETWORKING EVENTS

Long- Term Goal: _____

_____

Short-Term Goals: _____

_____

_____

_____

_____

Long-Term Goal: _____

_____

Short-Term Goals: _____

_____

_____

_____

FOCUS CALENDAR

...FOCUS CALENDAR...

Month: _____

My Goal for this Month is: _____

This Week I Will **Focus On**...				
MONDAY	○	○	○	○
TUESDAY	○	○	○	○
WEDNESDAY	○	○	○	○
THURSDAY	○	○	○	○
FRIDAY	○	○	○	○
SATURDAY	○	○	○	○
SUNDAY	○	○	○	○
Did I accomplish my tasks for this week? What did I learn this week and how can I improve?				

The Focus Calendar may remind you of a school planner, but what's different about the Focus Calendar is that it asks you to reflect on your progress at the end of each week. As you've learned in the previous chapters, one of the keys to achieving your goals and creating the life you want to live is by writing things down.

Complete your Focus Calendar for this month. At the beginning of each week, you have the option to pair up with someone and share how your week went. Talk about what tasks you completed as well what you learned and how you can improve. Prior to sharing with your partner let them know if you would like feedback or if you only want to share with no feedback. Feedback is helpful because you get another person's perspective and they may be able to notice things you missed or have suggestions you had not considered before.

When it's your turn to give feedback, please do so with respect and honesty as you would want the same done for you.

You may download and print extra copies of the Focus Calendar for FREE by going to www.VidaEsOro.org

Week 1 Reflections – What tasks did I complete? What did I learn? How can I improve? Did I receive feedback from a partner? If yes, what suggestions were useful to me?

_____

_____

_____

_____

_____

_____

_____

Week 2 Reflections – What tasks did I complete? What did I learn? How can I improve? Did I receive feedback from a partner? If yes, what suggestions were useful to me?

Week 3 Reflections – What tasks did I complete? What did I learn? How can I improve? Did I receive feedback from a partner? If yes, what suggestions were useful to me?

_____

_____

_____

_____

_____

_____

_____

_____

_____

_____

_____

_____

Week 4 Reflections – What tasks did I complete? What did I learn? How can I improve? Did I receive feedback from a partner? If yes, what suggestions were useful to me?

_____

_____

_____

EDUCATION

As I mentioned in this chapter, not every subject in school was my favorite, but I wanted to put forth 100% effort in order to pass my classes. How students feel about school ranges from, "I love school," "School is okay," and "I hate school." No matter your feelings towards school, a lesson you may take from your experience during this time is: there is something to be learned everyday that can create growth in your life, but you have to keep an open mind in order to receive it.

Something I had to learn was that I don't know everything and there are some things I don't understand or learn as fast as other people. And you know what…that's okay. I would ask questions and connect with others who did understand a concept and learn from them.

Exercise: Write down at least one thing you learned in each of your classes this week and one thing that you may not quite understand yet.

The purpose here is to be honest with yourself; it's one important way to improve.

Class title:_____

Something I learned this week:_____

_____

Something I don't understand yet:_____

_____

Class title:_____

Something I learned this week:_____

_____

Something I don't understand yet:_____

_____

Class title: _____

Something I learned this week: _____

_____

Something I don't understand yet: _____

_____

Class title: _____

Something I learned this week: _____

_____

Something I don't understand yet: _____

_____

Education can come in many forms. Majority of the time we think we have to be in a classroom to be learning. However, learning can also happen outside of the classroom by reading, taking online classes, volunteering, hands on experiences, etc.

Complete the sentence below to explain why learning is valuable to you.

I value learning because_____

_____

_____

ACCOUNTABILITY

Think of a time when you felt you did something "wrong" or you were told that you were "wrong?" How did that make you feel? What did you learn from that experience?

_____

_____

_____

_____

_____

_____

_____

_____

_____

_____

_____

_____

_____

Now that you've read this chapter, you know that learning comes from our mistakes, or rather the lessons we've experienced. The key is to use what we've learned to create positive results the next time we're in the same position.

In this chapter we also learned what it means to step outside of our comfort zone. Sometimes we stay in our comfort zone because we're afraid of change or we fear trying something new because we assume we're not going to do it "right." Yes, I understand that trying something new can be scary and we play mind games on ourselves by only coming up with all the bad things that may happen.

Think back to a time when you tried something new. Did you get it right the first time? What happened after you kept trying or practicing? Did you eventually get the hang of it? Are you now able to teach someone else how to do it and share the knowledge you've gained?

Write about an experience when you stepped outside of your comfort zone for the first time? How did you feel? What did you learn from the first time you tried it?

_____

_____

_____

_____

_____

_____

_____

_____

_____

_____

_____

_____

_____

_____

_____

The next time you get a little scared about trying something new, think back to a time when you overcame that fear and it turned out great for you.

Another part of being accountable is being responsible for our actions. Sometimes this may not be so easy to do because our first reaction may be to blame others when things don't go our way.

Write about an experience when something didn't go your way and you blamed someone else for what happened. Who did you blame? Why did blame them? Before blaming them, did you ask yourself if your actions had anything to do with the result that took place? What could you have done differently to see a different result?

_____

_____

_____

_____

_____

_____

_____

_____

_____
_____
_____
_____
_____
_____
_____

For the next 3 days, take notice of when you took responsibility for your actions. How did the experience begin? What were your thoughts and feelings? Did you initially have thoughts of blame or did you immediately take responsibility? Who was involved? Did you remain in control of your emotions or did you allow the situation to dictate your actions? How did you move forward? How do you feel about the situation now?

Day 1:_____
_____
_____
_____
_____
_____
_____
_____
_____

_____

_____

_____

Day 2:_____

_____

_____

_____

_____

_____

_____

_____

_____

_____

_____

Day 3:_____

_____

_____

_____

_____

_____

_____

_____

_____

_____

_____

_____

_____

_____

Now that you have an idea of what it means to be accountable, you also have several experiences to share when you took accountability for your actions.

Being accountable is taking responsibility for the things that only YOU can control.

BEING COACHABLE

Being coachable is an important trait to have because it allows you to be open to new ways of doing things in order to improve in all areas of your life.

Think of a time when you were given new information by someone who cares about you and wanted to see you improve. Did you immediately feel resistant towards listening or were you instantly open to learning something new? Did you end up taking none, a little, or all of their advice? Did you give 100% effort in your actions to improving? What was the result of it? Write about this experience.

_____

_____

_____

_____

_____

_____

_____

_____

_____

_____

Does being coachable sound similar to being open-minded? Yes. Now that you've become more clear on the importance of being coachable, complete the following exercise. For the next 3 days write about one experience each day when you were/were not being coachable or open-minded to something new. How did you respond? What was the result of each experience?

Day 1: _____

_____

_____

_____

_____

_____

_____

Day 2: _____

_____

_____

_____

_____

_____

Day 3: _____

_____

_____

KNOW YOUR WORTH

Complete the equation below to find out how much you're worth in the weight of gold.

At the time this book was written, the gold price per troy ounce averaged $1,220. 1 pound is equal to 14.58 troy ounce.

Multiply your body weight (lbs.) **(Insert your body weight)** lbs. x 14.58 = _____ t oz.
Example: 130 lbs. x 14.58 = 1,895.4 t oz.

Multiply your body weight in troy ounce **(Insert answer from above)** x $1,220 = $_____

Example: 1,895.4 t oz. x $1,220 = $2,312,388.00

In this example, I am worth over 2 million dollars in the weight of gold!

Insert how much you're worth in the weight of gold.

I AM WORTH $_____
(Disclaimer: This equation is only an example of where you can begin to find your value. The amount does not represent the true value of who you are, but it's a start.)

In the space below write down what it means to know your worth, which is also known as self-love. You may also work with a partner or group to share and listen to others describe what their worth means to them. You may want to add some of their thoughts to your definition.

_____

_____

_____

_____

___

___

___

Take a moment to write down some of the actions you take that show how much you love yourself. (Examples: going to the gym, taking a nap, spa day, trying something new, volunteering, removing yourself from a toxic situation, etc.)

___

___

___

___

Take a moment to write down some actions that you may want to take that show more self-love.

___

___

___

___

The more actions and decisions you make towards loving yourself, the more you will begin to feel more happiness and love internally, and you'll see it being created externally as well. How do you see and value yourself? When you put a high value on yourself, your actions and decisions will be a reflection of it.

MENTAL TOUGHNESS

In this chapter you learned that being in control of your emotions and actions is important so that you'll always put yourself in a position that will be beneficial for you. Making good decisions in emotional moments is essential to your success.

Think of a time when you allowed your emotions to control your actions. Write down what happened and who was involved. What led you to react in a way where you were not in control? What was the result of this interaction? What did you learn from this experience?

_____

_____

_____

_____

_____

_____

_____

_____

_____

_____

Write down an experience you had when you overcame adversity. How did you feel when the challenge arose? Were you happy, excited sad, frustrated or hurt? Did you initially want to give up or keep going? How did you determine the path you were going to take? Did you have to shift your mindset at any point in order to overcome the challenge?

_____
_____
_____
_____
_____
_____
_____
_____
_____
_____
_____
_____
_____

It's in the moments when you feel tired, frustrated or even defeated, that you remind yourself of why you give 100% effort to attain your goals. You control YOU, so be in control of YOU.

Your mental strength will give you the physical strength to keep moving forward. It will give you motivation to overcome any negative thoughts or emotions you may have and be the fuel that your body and mind need to reach your goals.

Asking for support is one of the most beneficial things we can do for ourselves in order to continue to learn and grow to become better versions of ourselves. Sometimes asking for help may seem intimidating because we think we're not smart enough. Other times we may wonder if people will judge us or criticize us. Or maybe we think people are too busy and we don't want to bother them by asking for help.

Many times we're already assuming the worst before we even ask a person for help and the majority of the time the person we want to ask is not thinking or feeling any of those negative emotions that we've made up in our mind.

Do you see how powerful the mind is? We can make something up that's not true about someone else and actually believe it! This is another part of being mentally tough in how you communicate with yourself and others. Do you assume or do you go directly to the person and communicate with them?

Answer the following questions:

1. **Do you feel comfortable asking for help? Why or why not?**

_____

_____

_____

_____

_____

2. Write about a time when you were afraid to ask for help or you made up a story in your head as to why you didn't want to ask for help even though you knew you needed it. What was the result of your decision? How did the outcome make you feel?

_____
_____
_____
_____
_____
_____
_____
_____
_____

3. Write about an experience when you did ask for help. What did you need help with? How did you feel when you asked for help? What did you learn from this experience?

_____
_____
_____
_____
_____
_____

CHARACTER COUNTS

Your character is a reflection of your self-worth.

In the exercise below, you'll see the letters A, B, and C. Each letter is going to represent someone who you have recently shown a lack of respect towards. You don't have to write their names down, only remember who represents each letter. In each section write down what you did to show a lack of respect. How did this make you feel? How can you improve on how you treat each of these individuals?

Person A:_____

_____

_____

_____

_____

_____

_____

Person B:_____

_____

_____

_____

_____

_____

_____

Person C:_____

_____

_____

_____

_____

_____

_____

_____

Write 10 character traits that describe who you are. For each characteristic you wrote down, circle yes or no next to it if you display this characteristic everyday. It's okay if you don't, this is about you being honest with yourself. This is how you learn, grow and improve.

1._____   Yes   No

2._____   Yes   No

3._____   Yes   No

4._____   Yes   No

5._____   Yes   No

6._____   Yes   No

7._____   Yes   No

8._____   Yes   No

9._____   Yes   No

10._____   Yes   No

Our character is not only a representation of how we treat ourselves, but also how we treat others. Have you experienced a moment when you became frustrated by someone's actions or felt hurt by something they did? Were you aware of your emotions before you acted? Or did you want to retaliate, thinking it would make you feel better? Although, it may make you feel better in the initial moment, retaliating doesn't solve the problem in the long run. Your hurt and frustration will more than likely come up again for you. This goes back to mental toughness and being in control of your emotions and actions.

Gratitude:
Gratitude is a form of appreciation in being grateful for what you have in this present moment without comparing it to what you feel you don't have. Saying thank you goes a long way, similar to the way a smile can positively impact someone's day. Showing gratitude is not only an action, but it carries a positive emotion with it as well. The person receiving the gratitude and the person giving the gratitude both feel the appreciation through the interaction.

For the next 5 days you're going to write down 5 things you were grateful for each day. At the end of each day, allow yourself time to reflect and you may begin to see and realize there are many great things happening to you everyday.

Day 1: Today I am grateful for…

1._____

2._____

3._____

4._____

5._____

Day 2: Today I am grateful for…

1._____

2._____

3._____

4._____

5._____

Day 3: Today I am grateful for…

1._____

2._____

3._____

4._____

5._____

Day 4: Today I am grateful for…

1._____

2._____

3._____

4._____

5._____

Day 5: Today I am grateful for…

1._____

2._____

3._____

4._____

5._____

Think of 3 people who have made a huge impact on your life. Sometimes we take people for granted with the impact they've made on us and we miss out on the opportunity in sharing our gratitude with them. Maybe it's the words or actions someone showed towards you and you didn't realize the impact they had on you, but now you realize it.

Below you're going to see the letters A, B, and C and each letter is going to represent the 3 people you thought of. You don't have to write their names down, only remember who represents each letter. This is an opportunity for you to recognize each individual. This can be in the form of a letter, email, phone call, or in-person conversation. Be sure to allow yourself the time to write something to them or speak to them, so that you don't feel rushed and can truly embrace the experience.

Write down the form of communication you used to share your gratitude and write about how you felt when you shared your appreciation.

Person A – Form of communication used:_____

What did you say and how did you feel? _____

_____

_____

_____

_____

Person B – Form of communication used:_____

What did you say and how did you feel? _____

_____

_____

_____

_____

Person C – Form of communication used: _____

What did you say and how did you feel? _____

_____

_____

_____

_____

BELIEVE

Continue to put effort into improving the skills necessary to achieve your goals and you'll begin to notice the progress you make. As a result, your belief in yourself will grow. Believing in yourself is a powerful tool towards achieving your goals.

With the foundation of self-worth, which includes the components of mental toughness, great character and belief in yourself, added with the goals that motivate you, being accountable and coachable, you will have the recipe for achieving anything you set your mind to.

Describe the vision you have for your life. Include all the details as to what the life you are creating looks like. Close your eyes for a bit and visualize it all. The reason you're writing it down is because the power is in your words. You can always come back to this workbook and remind yourself of the significance your "Why" has on your life.

_____

_____

_____

_____

_____

_____

_____

_____

_____

_____

_____

_____

_____

_____

_____

_____

The decision to create your life is yours and it begins with your mind. Take action!

Treasure Yourself & Shine!

Made in the USA
Columbia, SC
09 March 2024

32389702R00026